The Fires of York Minster

From AD 741 to 9 July 1984

The Fires of York Minster

The Early Fires

In the year 741, exactly a century after York's first stone cathedral, begun in 627, was completed, Simeon of Durham records that 'the Minster in the city of York was burnt on Sunday 23rd May'. In 867, in the course of the Viking raids on England, the same chronicler records that 'an innumerable host of barbarians came to England by sea and devastated everything with fire and the sword; the abominable army of the Danes moved from East Anglia to the city of York on All Saints' Day; they came to York and attacked the city, devastating it all round; at length, having entered the city, they engaged in a very disastrous battle on Palm Sunday.'

In 1069, in the aftermath of the Norman conquest, the people of York dared to oppose the rule of King William and paid dearly for their resistance. In the words of Hugh Sottowain, chantor of the Minster, 'The city of York was destroyed by the French with sword, famine, and flames; the metropolitan church of St Peter was also burned, and its ornaments, charters, and privileges consumed or lost.' Some additional details are supplied by the chronicler Florentius of Worcester: 'On Saturday the 13th of the kalends of October [19 September] the Normans set fire to the houses adjacent to the castle, and the flames spread and attacked the whole of the city and entirely consumed it, together with the Minster of St Peter.'

In 1137 the Norman Minster, begun by Archbishop Thomas of Bayeux about 1080 after the burning of the Saxon building in 1069, suffered in an accidental fire which ravaged much of the city. According to an anonymous continuation of the chronicle of Florentius of Worcester, written probably at Gloucester around 1150, not many years after the event, when this destruction must still have been a vivid memory (here quoted from the unpublished Elizabethan translation of Raphael Holinshed), 'This year [1137] many churches were burnt, Saint Peter's church, the archbishop's see in York, the second of the nones of June [4 June] and our lady Mary's church where there was an abbey, with the hospital in the same city the same day, with thirty-nine other churches, also the Trinity church in the suburbs of the city.' The choir of the Minster was duly rebuilt on a larger scale by Archbishop Roger, about 1155–75. In 1463–4, the third year of the reign of King Edward IV, Bishop Francis Godwin, in his life of Archbishop William Bothe, records that 'the Minster of York was burnt, I know not by what chance.' Perhaps it is this occasion which is referred to in a visitation record of the Minster in 1519, which mentions 'a goodly well in the crowdes [i.e. the crypt], which hath been used in old time and did great good when the church was burned; it wanteth nothing but a pulley and a rope, and the door of the same is kept locked.' This is the earliest record of any form of fire-fighting in the Minster.

In the middle of the 18th century both lightning and fire attacked the Minster. 'In 1745 the large south-east pinnacle was thrown down by lightning, and the prodigious stones which composed it carried to a considerable distance: another was soon after erected in its place, in every respect equal to the former.' 'In 1753 an accident happened, which was near proving fatal to this noble edifice, and threatened to lay all its honours in the dust. By carelessness of the workmen a chafing-dish of coals, which was used in fixing the lead upon the roof, had been left by them in one of the lead gutters, and by the heat of the coals the wood under the lead, which was extremely dry, took fire, and blazed out with great rapidity before it was discovered: as soon as it was observed, which was about eight o'clock in the evening, the inhabitants of the city were in the utmost consternation, and ran from all quarters to assist in extinguishing the flames; which, by the means of a number of fire-engines, was happily effected, after burning a considerable part of the roof over the little aisle in the south cross. The damage occasioned by this fire was, with great diligence, repaired by the active care of the present dean [John Fountayne].' The accounts show the expenditure of £3. 11s. 'for drink etc. when the fire in

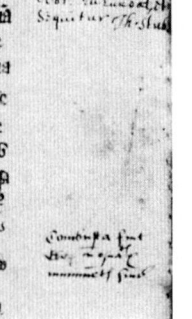

the Minster was extinguished'. In the following year a fire engine and buckets were bought in London for £24. 17s. They were brought to York by sea, and freight and crane dues at the wharf on the Ouse cost a further £1. 2s. 6d. This is the earliest fire-fighting equipment at the Minster. In 1806 a more modern, more sophisticated, larger and more expensive fire engine was bought from Messrs Hadley and Simpkin of Long Acre, London. Their basic 'Anne Patent 6th size Fire Engine with a Copper Branch and Suction Pipe compleat' cost £85, and supplementary equipment and associated costs brought the total bill to £150. 9s.

The 19th-Century Fires

The 19th and 20th centuries have seen a number of outbreaks of fire in various parts of the Minster. Most of these were quickly extinguished and therefore received little publicity. There were, however, two outbreaks before 1984 which became major conflagrations. In 1829 Jonathan Martin, acting, he claimed, in obedience to a vision, set fire to the Minster, destroying the choir roof, the organ, the medieval stalls and all the furnishings of the eastern section of the building. It was a spectacular conflagration. An eyewitness remarked that the sight recalled one of the vast biblical scenes painted by the popular artist John Martin, not knowing that as he said this he was watching the work of the artist's brother.

★

FACING PAGE, ABOVE: *Lines from a 14th-century manuscript in the York Minster archives containing Hugh the Chantor's account of the fire which consumed the Saxon Minster in 1069.*

FACING PAGE, BELOW: *The original visitation record of 1519 mentioning the well in the crypt of the Minster which had been used for fighting a fire, probably in 1464.*

RIGHT: *Part of a contemporary engraving showing on the left the south-eastern pinnacle which was struck by lightning in 1745. It was repaired after this, then again in 1836 after the fire of 1829, and for a third time in 1984 after gale damage.*

TOP: *An 1824 Leeds and Yorkshire fire engine used by Bridlington Corporation. It required two teams of 32 men to pump in five-minute shifts. Bystanders would be enlisted to help, and were paid in beer tokens. York Castle Museum.*

LEFT: *Jonathan Martin, who set fire to the Minster in 1829.*

ABOVE: *Medallion commemorating the 1829 fire.*

FACING PAGE: *'View of the interior of York Minster as it appeared immediately after the roof fell in on the morning of the 2nd February 1829', as drawn by John Browne.*

Jonathan Martin was afflicted by a form of religious mania known as 'ranting'. At his confirmation he was, he said, 'astonished at the wonderful size of the bishop', and ascribed such corpulence to the effect of drinking too much wine. Later, he alarmed the congregation of his parish church and angered the incumbent by hiding in the pulpit before the service and rising unexpectedly after the psalms to address the people.

During January 1829 he made frequent visits to the Minster, leaving messages pinned to the choir gates. In these he denounced the Dean and Chapter for their bottles of wine, their roast beef and plum puddings. 'You whitent sea pulkirs … your Gret Charchis and Minstairs will cume rattling down upon your Gilty Heads.' At the time no one paid much attention, and it was only at the inquest after the fire that these words took on a dreadful significance.

On Sunday 1 February 1829, Jonathan Martin attended Evensong. Although he was by now a familiar figure to the vergers, they had no reason to suspect the purpose of his visit. He was in some excitement, he later recalled, at the prospect of executing a divine instruction to destroy the cathedral, and he said that it was the organ in particular that evening which seemed to manifest the devil. 'I'll have thee down tonight', he muttered, 'thou shalt buzz no more.' After Evensong he hid behind a tomb until the cathedral was locked and he was able to set about his work undisturbed.

When the fire was discovered the next morning it had been burning slowly for at least five hours. At first it was thought to be manageable, and the Minster fire engine was wheeled from the vestry to subdue the flames, but it proved to be wholly ineffective, as did the city firemen, a crew of elderly and incapacitated men who lived in cottages dispersed across the town with 'Fireman' inscribed on boards above their doors.

It was not till Major Clark arrived with a detachment of the 7th Dragoon Guards and their own engine that matters fell into more capable hands. By now the great organ had caught alight. Burning fiercely for some time, it finally gave out a ghastly groan before perishing in the flames. As the fire got hold of the roof, the private fire engine of Mr Beilby Thompson MP arrived from Escrick Park, drawn by four handsome grey carriage horses. At about the same time the engines from Leeds began to arrive. The first reached York after a journey of two hours; the second was delayed by the loss of a wheel; the third lost a horse, the poor creature dropping dead on the way; and the fourth overturned as it rounded the corner into Minster Yard.

Despite the great courage of the firemen, some of whom had tried to hack the burning roof timbers away from the gable to protect the great east window, it was the collapse of the choir roof which saved the rest of the building from destruction. Jane Thomas wrote about the event three days later to her friend Miss Armitage: 'I went at nine in the morning and did not quit the spot till near two. At about eleven despair seemed to take possession of every mind for it was the general opinion that the whole building must inevitably be lost, but we ought to be very thankful that the fire was turned from the large tower as soon as the roof of the east end fell in, which took place about twelve o'clock.'

At his trial, when he behaved with great composure and dignity, Jonathan Martin was found not guilty on the grounds of insanity. It was a verdict which the Dean and Chapter had hoped for, as they had no mind to see him hang. The public, however, was less charitable and felt cheated. A small souvenir medallion was struck, on which the incendiary was depicted in three positions: standing free, sitting in chains and hanging from the gallows. Beneath were inscribed the words: 'What I was. What I am. What I ought to be.' But outweighing these vengeful sentiments were those of grief as the city mourned the disfigurement of her noblest house. It was a sorrow summed up in the words of Isaiah 64, which by chance were due to be read at Evensong the Sunday following the fire:

> Our holy and our beautiful house, where our fathers praised thee, is burned up with fire: and all our pleasant things are laid waste.

On the evening of 20 May 1840, at a quarter to nine, passers-by saw a light in the south-west tower. A workman had accidentally left a burning candle in the chamber beneath the bells, and it was not long before the flames had spread through the tower. Within minutes of the flames first being seen, the alarm spread through the city, bringing a great crowd to witness the second conflagration at the Minster within 11 years.

Thomas Marshall, Constable of the Liberty of St Peter, was one of the first to see the fire. He went to fetch a bucket of water, but when he reached the door of the south-west tower he found it locked and could not get into the building. When the news reached the Lord Mayor, who was attending a meeting of the York Operative Protestants Association in the Festival Concert Room, he immediately ordered the despatch of an express railway train to fetch fire engines from Leeds. These arrived in due course to supplement the work of the engines

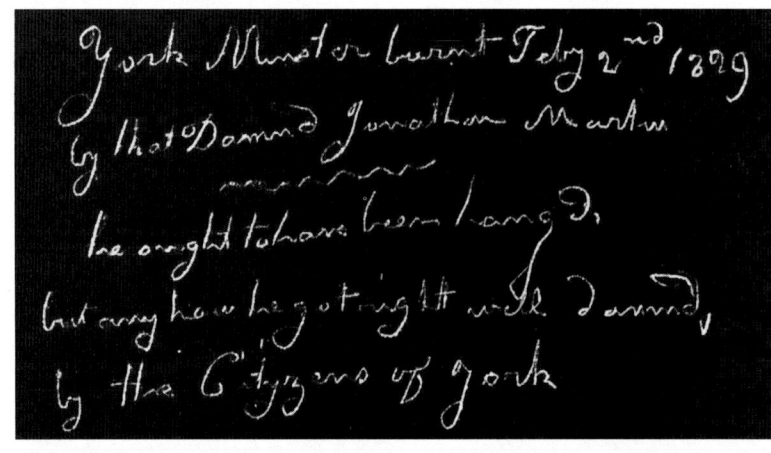

which had been sent by the insurance companies, by the military and by Lord Wenlock of Escrick Park. Although the engines of the Yorkshire Insurance Company and the North of England Insurance Company were soon on the spot, it was 20 minutes before the engine of the Waterworks Company could get up sufficient steam to pump water into the mains. However, when the water began to flow it did so abundantly, 240,000 gallons being the estimated quantity.

The Dragoon Guards and a troop of mounted Hussars were sent for by the Lord Mayor, and during the night, together with the police and members of the York Militia, they kept the large crowds from approaching the building. An eyewitness described how 'the clanking of the engines and the hoarse voices of the firemen, with the glittering sabres of the military and the reflection of the flames upon the assembled crowd heightened the scene'. A more frightening sound was soon heard above the clanking of the engines, for as the fire consumed the timbers within the tower the peal of ten bells began to crash one by one to the ground below, carrying with them fragments of the intervening floors and sending into the night above sheets of vivid flame.

By 11 p.m. the fire seemed to have been brought under control, and people believed that the building had been saved. However, smoke was then seen rising from the nave roof, and soon flames confirmed everyone's fears. As the timber vault of the great nave was engulfed by fire, eyewitnesses believed that the entire building would be destroyed, and books and ornaments were hurriedly removed from the choir. The ancient muniments of the Dean and Chapter and the records of the Diocesan Registry were passed from the building by a chain of people and conveyed by hackney carriage under military escort to the Monkgate residence of Mr Buckle, the Registrar. Fortunately these precautions were unnecessary, for, as it had done in 1829 and as it would do again in 1984, the massive bulk of the central tower halted the advance of the flames and saved the building.

In 1899 Dean Purey Cust wrote, 'Persons still living remember the

★

FACING PAGE: *Scratched on a window by a workman in a part of the Minster inaccessible to the public, this inscription shows the feeling of the ordinary York people in 1829.*

ABOVE: *A contemporary view of the night of the 1840 fire, showing cavalrymen holding back the crowds of sightseers.*

7

terrifying incidents of that awful night, how as children they were carried from their beds out of the surrounding houses lest the blazing towers should fall upon them, and how, when the great roof fell and a sudden glare of fire lit up the smoke and darkness within, the great crucifix in the West window of the South aisle shone out distinct and beautiful, and the cordon of soldiers, which surrounded the building to keep back the crowds, involuntarily raised their right hands and saluted.'

The 1984 Fire

At 2.30 a.m. on the morning of Monday 9 July 1984 the alarm sounded in the Minster and in the York Fire Station. Within minutes both the Fire Brigade and the police arrived at the scene.

However, despite this swift response, the fire had already got a strong hold, having spread silently and unseen through the dry timbers of the huge roof space before eventually setting off the automatic alarms.

Many witnesses later recalled seeing a lightning storm over York that night. Guests at an 18th-birthday party four miles away in Huntington watched the storm flickering and flashing over the city centre. Among them was the daughter of one of the Minster clergy who, as she cycled home in the early hours, could not guess the cause of the vivid orange glow in the sky – until she turned into the cathedral precincts. Her feelings of appalled incredulity at the sight of the blazing building were shared by the other residents of the Minster Close who were now being awoken by the hurrying footsteps and shouts of the firemen and the growing glare of the flames.

The officer in charge in the early stages of the fire could see at once that the fire was well established in the roof and had penetrated downwards through the vaulting. Firemen wearing breathing apparatus sets, and carrying ropes to enable them to haul hose lines to the roof, were detailed to set off up the narrow spiral stairs. The 100-foot ladder was being made stable outside the Minster and as soon as possible it would be raised to its fullest extent. Other firemen were laying out hoses to the water mains. Everyone was busy and more help was needed. The call went out for more appliances.

Meanwhile, the firemen sent to climb the staircase failed to reach the roof, owing to locked doors and the intense heat. Other crews had,

however, reached the roof by Fire Brigade ladders, and hose lines were being brought into place. Two more fire engines were requested and information about the nature of the fire was given to Brigade Control. More fire engines were mobilised to close in on York in anticipation of further requests for assistance.

Several hose lines were now working at roof level and the famous rose window was being cooled by water sprayed on the stonework above, but the fire was still spreading. Molten lead and debris were falling within the south transept, making conditions at ground level hazardous. A York crew had forced their way through a maintenance door

★

FACING PAGE: *Fire-fighting at the height of the 1984 blaze.*

ABOVE: *Flames sweeping through the south transept, illuminating the rose window from inside.*

giving access to the space between the roof and the vaulting. They were met by massive burning but they knew that this was the best place to fight the fire. Restricted by the confines of the space and the tangle of supporting timbers, they played their hoses from the doorway but found that the bow of the vaulting was deflecting the water stream away from the fire. They persevered, but the fire was still spreading. Meanwhile, Fire Brigade ladders had been pitched in stages up the differing roof levels of the Minster to give a continuous external staircase from ground to roof on both sides of the south transept. A water cannon was working from the floor of the transept and a massive jet of water was reaching up towards the fire from underneath. All these tasks needed men. Control was asked to send four more engines.

Meanwhile, the Dean and Mrs Jasper were leading a small group of clergy and other residents in rescuing from the smoke-filled building all the portable furnishings and ornaments of

value that they could carry. Soon the Chapter House Yard became piled with crosses and candlesticks from six altars, rugs and large carpets, curtains, frontals, tapestry kneelers and books. In again they went, some with wet handkerchiefs in front of their faces, until forced back by the intensity of the smoke and the falling debris.

Conditions for the firemen in the doorway were now also becoming unbearable. Where they were working, the vaulting had become unstable and several large pieces had crashed to the transept floor. Reluctantly, they were withdrawn to the parapet. It was clear that there was no chance of saving the transept roof. More jets were brought into operation to continue to protect the central tower, and water lines were laid from the River Ouse.

The question was, how far the fire could be contained. The transept had chapels to the east and west with timber roofs open at clerestory level to the south transept. The fire must not be allowed to spread into these. It would also be possible for the fire to spread across the corners where the transept joined the nave and choir. The main worry, however, was the central tower. This squarely adjoins the south transept and has large leaded windows overlooking the transept roof. Like the south transept, the vaulting and roof of the central tower are constructed of timber. Because of its height above the main cathedral, it was an obvious collecting area for the heat generated by the fire. The only access is by a narrow spiral staircase starting from the south transept roof. Several attempts to reach the tower roof had failed. Hose lines had been mounted at all the crucial points but, because of its height, it was not possible to protect the arch. The leaded windows had a built-in vulnerability. A tongue of flame passing under the arch, or fire passing through the leaded windows, would soon cause what one man called 'the biggest chimney fire ever seen'. In spite of the amount of water being applied, the fire was still burning nearer and nearer to the central tower. Water striking the outside of the roof was running off with little of it reaching the fire, and no matter how jets were angled it seemed impossible to get enough water into the space between the roof and the vaulting to extinguish the flames.

Five more engines were requested. The only chance was to try to pull, or push, as much burning material as possible down from the roof and away from the tower. All the main roof supports were still in position but several had been severely weakened by the fire. The water was directed at the side of the weakened beams. Like a row of dominoes, progressive collapse spread along the roof until it was stopped by the stronger, unburnt timbers nearer the central tower. The weight of the falling structure then took charge and dragged the remainder of the roof clear of the tower and down to the floor of the transept.

To watch this happening was an awesome, even terrifying sight. Would the stonework stand the strain? How solid was the central tower? Would the falling roof pull with it the gable and the rose window? What about the safety of Fire Brigade personnel? Although a check had been carried out to make sure that no one was within the south transept, firemen were still at work at roof level when the collapse occurred. Not readily noticed by the visitor is the fact that the lead roof-covering is lapped under the lead covering the parapets, often for a considerable distance. Many of the firemen had the

★

LEFT: *From the top of the 100-foot ladder a fireman tries to cool the rose window by spraying the stonework above it, while others work to contain the blaze at roof level.*

FACING PAGE: *The morning light filters through the dense smoke filling the central tower.*

PAGE 12: *Two dramatic photographs of the 1984 fire, showing the flames leaping as high as the central tower and the framework of the roof highlighted against the burning vault.*

PAGE 13: *The south transept in flames, photographed by a visitor to York from the window of his hotel room in the centre of the city.*

sensation of the floor under their feet moving as the roof collapsed. One fireman who finished spread-eagled on a stone balustrade described the effect as totally frightening and the noise as totally deafening.

The roof collapsed at about 3.45 a.m. and this was the turning point of the crisis, for once the roof material was on the floor, it was possible to extinguish the flames and concentrate on checking that the fire had not spread in any way into the remainder of the Minster. This was a particularly difficult task, for the nave and choir and the central tower were all filled with a dense pall of smoke which extended downwards from the ceiling almost to floor level. Fire crews were in attendance at the Minster for approximately 24 hours, dealing with minor outbreaks and undertaking extensive salvage operations, including pumping out gallons of water from the Undercroft below the central tower.

The Cause: Was it Lightning?

The fire left an aftermath of impressions as confused as the blackened wreckage on the floor of the transept. But very quickly the Fire Brigade, whose job it was to assess the cause, began asking questions, sifting the debris and taking statements from witnesses before memories became distorted by the impact of a dramatic event.

In determining the cause of a fire, investigators seek to establish the area where the fire originated and then look for the possible causes of fire in that location. In the case of the fire in the south transept, the area of origin was known because flames were seen discharging from above and below it. Therefore, the main question to be answered related to the possible causes of ignition in that area. These were eventually identified as carelessly discarded smoking material; hazards introduced by maintenance workers; or a fault in electrical equipment.

Members of the public en route to the staircase leading to the top of the central lantern had to pass the area where the fire started. However, there was no public access to the roof void itself. Investigations revealed that the last member of the public to use the route to the top of the central lantern left the premises at 7.30 p.m. on the evening before the fire. Possibly cigarette ends were dropped by individuals, but these could hardly have set fire to the massive timbers of the roof void and, in any case, it was difficult to see how they could have come into direct contact with them.

Maintenance work, involving the use of blow torches and other hazardous equipment, has often caused fires, but no maintenance workers were in the Minster during the weekend and no such work had been carried out in

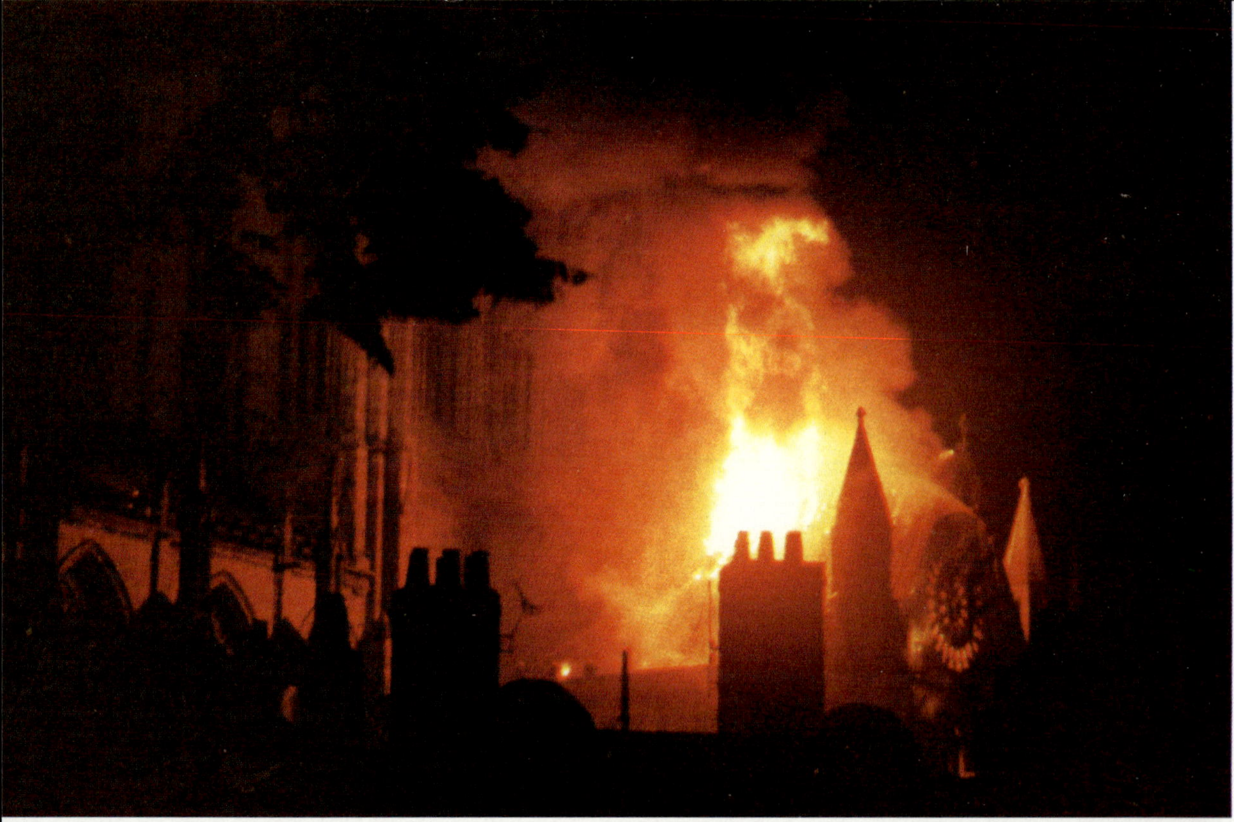

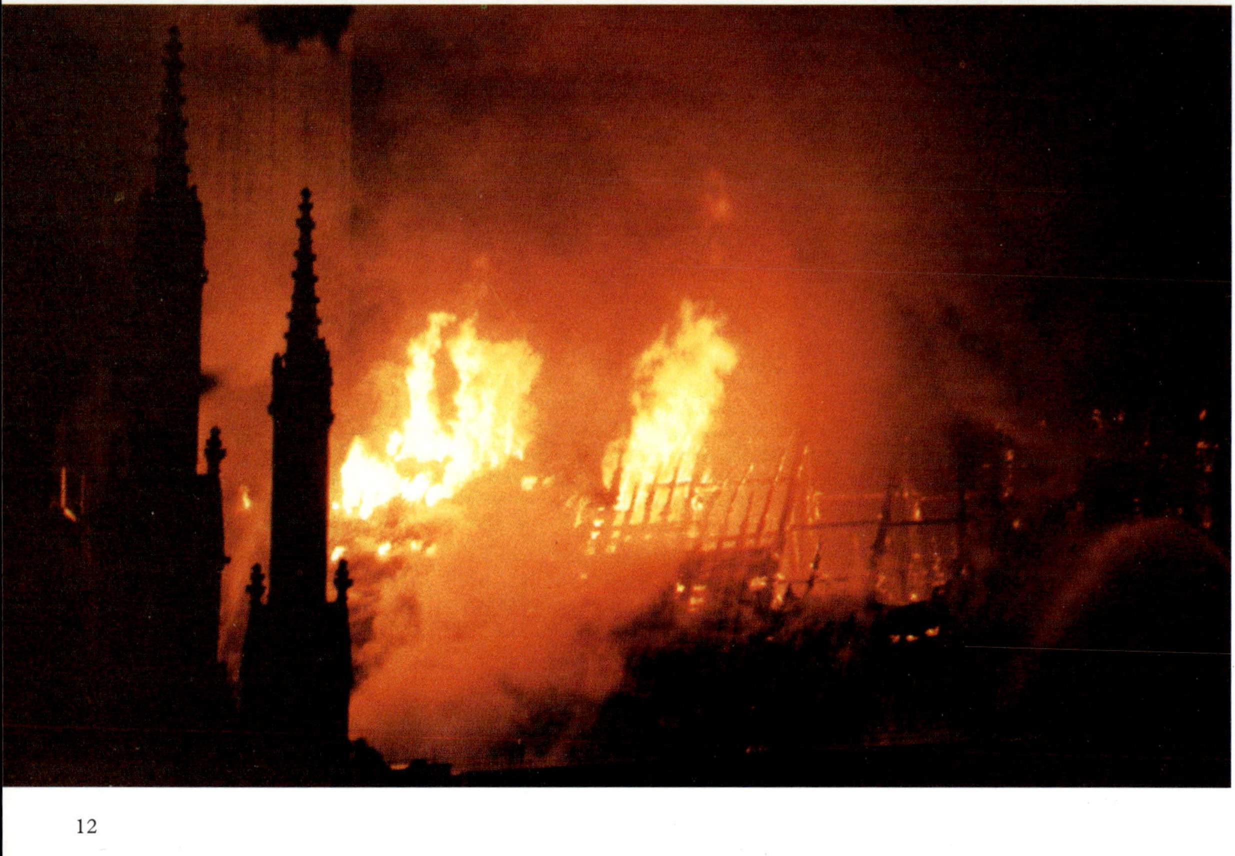

the south transept roof for many weeks. This possibility could therefore safely be dismissed.

The electrical equipment was looked at very carefully. The wiring was of a high standard, installed in earthed conduits throughout and therefore isolated from the timber. Any circuit fault would have been confined within the metal cladding and, in any case, the protective circuit breakers were found to have been activated, almost certainly as a result of the fire itself and not because of a fault. It was therefore decided that an electrical fault was not likely to have been the cause of the fire.

Since the preceding factors could be discounted, the possibility of arson had to be taken very seriously. However, despite the efforts of the country's senior Fire Brigade and Police officers, no clear evidence could be found to support arson as being the cause of the fire. Equally, the investigators were unable to find proof that the fire had not been started deliberately. But now we must consider the other important factor in the night's events.

The night of 8–9 July 1984 was hot, sultry and still; of the many witnesses to lightning flashes that night, none reported hearing thunder. This was the most curious aspect; lightning usually results in thunder, but it is possible that what was observed was actually 'corona', which always precedes lightning but which is seldom visible to the eye. Corona is less severe than lightning, but it has some properties in common with it.

Lightning is a hazard to all buildings, and a structure such as the Minster, standing above the surrounding city and plain, is especially vulnerable. Could lightning – or corona – have caused the

★

LEFT: *A fireman on the walkway after the collapse of the roof (above); molten lead hangs from the parapet (below).*

FACING PAGE: *Heroes of the blaze: exhausted firemen recuperate with a mug of tea, while in the lower right-hand picture is the coat of York Fire Brigade Commander Terry Earnshaw, with spots of molten lead on the shoulders.*

fire? This possibility was investigated carefully. Both phenomena are electric currents, and in each case the current increases rapidly in a very short time after its initiation, commonly at the rate of 10,000 million amperes per second in a few millionths of a second.

The Minster was protected by lightning conductors. The function of a lightning conductor, which protrudes above the highest point of a building, is to attract lightning and conduct electrical energy safely to earth. In so doing, a very high voltage – perhaps a million volts – could be developed at the top of each conductor due to the properties of inductance and resistance which result from the length of its route to the ground.

The south transept was equipped with two conductors on the gable-end wall and the whole of the lead roof was connected to them. This provided what appeared to be magnificent lightning protection covering the whole transept. But fixed to the wooden roof structure, just beneath the lead sheeting, were the electrical circuits in their conduits and metal control boxes, all of which were earthed. Thus, if a strike occurred either to the roof or to the lightning conductor system, the whole of that area would rise to perhaps a million volts, so that a heavy spark might occur between the roof and the earthed electrical equipment if they were not sufficiently separated. This is called 'sideflash'; it can splinter timber and start a fire.

Tests carried out at Leeds University simulated parts of the roof structure and showed that the most vulnerable part of the roof was at the small vestibule where a metal control box was mounted on timber. Here, less than 150,000 volts would have been needed to flash through the wood to the earthed box, and this could easily have been developed at the roof by the electrical activity above the building. A small blaze starting in the vestibule could then have convected upwards to the point at which it broke through and became visible six feet above.

It is in the nature of the event that evidence of this process would be destroyed in the fire, and positive proof is therefore lacking. However, sideflash is known to cause fire, and the many reports of electrical activity give support to the theory.

To sum up, then, what did cause the fire? Credibility and scientific arguments are stretched unreasonably by theories based on cigarette ends, lighted matches, long-departed maintenance men and so on. An electrical circuit fault seems most unlikely. Arson is more difficult to rule out – indeed, proof that arson did not occur is subject to the age-old problem of proving a negative. Electrical activity – lightning, corona and so on – is very plausible, and although no direct evidence survived the disaster, the circumstantial evidence is strong.

Perhaps we shall never be certain of the cause. The Fire Brigade report concluded that it was '80 per cent probable' that the fire was caused by lightning or some other atmospheric electrical activity. There was a 10 per cent possibility of arson and a further 10 per cent possibility of the fire being caused by an electrical fault. We can only reflect that this form of conclusion highlights the problem of weighing a set of unusual factors in trying to account for what was, by any standards, an improbable event – the fire of 9 July 1984.

15

Aftermath

The fire destroyed two quite separate structures, the roof and the vault below it. Although the roof was a timber structure of impressive proportions, it was a 'recent' (18th-century) addition to the south transept; the vault, however, was considerably older than the roof and of a most unusual type. Of the two structures destroyed, the vault was by far the greater loss to the Minster.

In a report to the Dean and Chapter in 1770, the architect John Carr had commented unfavourably upon the state of the late-medieval roof which was then still surviving. Accordingly, between 1744 and 1776 a new roof was built by one Leonard Terry. He faced a difficult task, for he had to design his roof trusses to pass over the vault, which intruded awkwardly into the roof space. His work, nonetheless, was successful, and when completed the new roof was covered with slates.

Just over a century later, from 1871 to 1880, the architect George Edmund Street carried out extensive repairs and consolidations to the south transept, and also to its roof. Street, concerned about the outward bulging of the transept walls, strengthened both the upper parts of the walls and Terry's roof. He, too, was confronted with the problem of the rising vault. To either side of Terry's great timber trusses, Street bolted long 'passing braces', beams which crossed over the vault below to resist further spreading of the roof. To reduce the load upon the walls, Street replaced the slates with lead, which made the roof somewhat lighter.

Although this outline of events is documented clearly enough in the Minster's archives, neither Terry nor Street left detailed drawings of their work; moreover, the restricted access within the roof-space caused by the close proximity of roof to vault meant that no subsequent full record could be made. Whilst the general arrangement

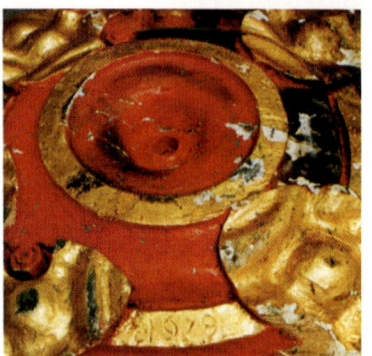

TOP: *16 July 1984: HRH The Duchess of Kent is shown the damage and the work of cleaning up after the fire, by the then Dean of York, the Very Reverend Ronald Jasper, and other members of the Minster staff.*

ABOVE: *One of the 16 bosses replaced in 1979 which survived the flames.*

FACING PAGE: *The south transept from the air, two days after the fire.*

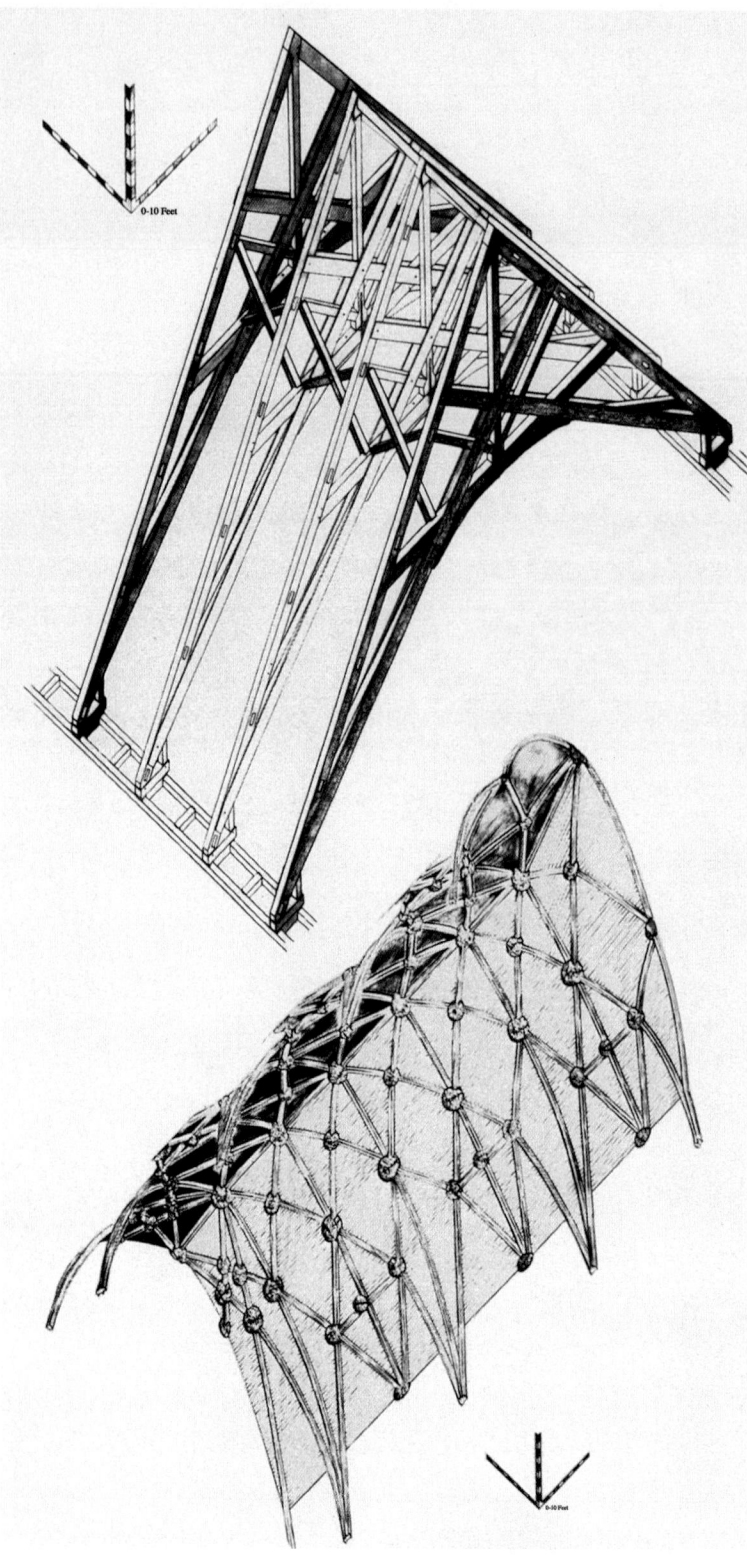

of the roof was understood well enough, there was, for example, no list of the types of joint used by the 18th-century carpenters.

The vault which caused such difficulty to Terry and Street was built in the early years of the 15th century to span the 13th-century transept upon the completion of the present central tower. It was a remarkable structure in that it was not a copy in wood of a stone vault, but an original design which exploited the structural possibilities of wood. The vault was self-supporting, with its ribs arranged in a 'net' or diamond pattern, a method of covering large spaces which has only been revived in the 20th century with the advent of modern building materials. The transept vault, therefore, was a remarkable demonstration of the 15th-century carpenter's sensitivity to the material with which he was working.

During the 19th-century restoration several of the oak boards that originally made up the web of the vault, and which had been hidden by a lath-and-plaster web of the late 18th-century, were uncovered. Street took these oak boards, decorated as they were with a single red line, as the model for the restored web of the vault. He completed the work of restoration by gilding the bosses on a ground of vermilion. There were 68 bosses, made of oak, marking the intersections of ribs which were also of oak. The ribs had been fashioned from trees specially selected to fit the desired curvature of

★

LEFT: *The 18th-century roof with the 'passing braces' added by G.E. Street: a drawing prepared in October 1984 following study of the burnt timbers (above). A reconstruction-study of the medieval 'net' vault, drawn in 1984 after the fire which destroyed it (below).*

FACING PAGE, ABOVE: *The debris on the morning of 9 July 1984. The tapes mark out a grid by which the individual timbers are located: this first stage in building up a record of the roof and vault was begun immediately the smoke had cleared. Note two gilded bosses in the foreground.*

FACING PAGE, BELOW: *Two days after the fire more than 1,000 timbers lie ready for the work of cataloguing.*

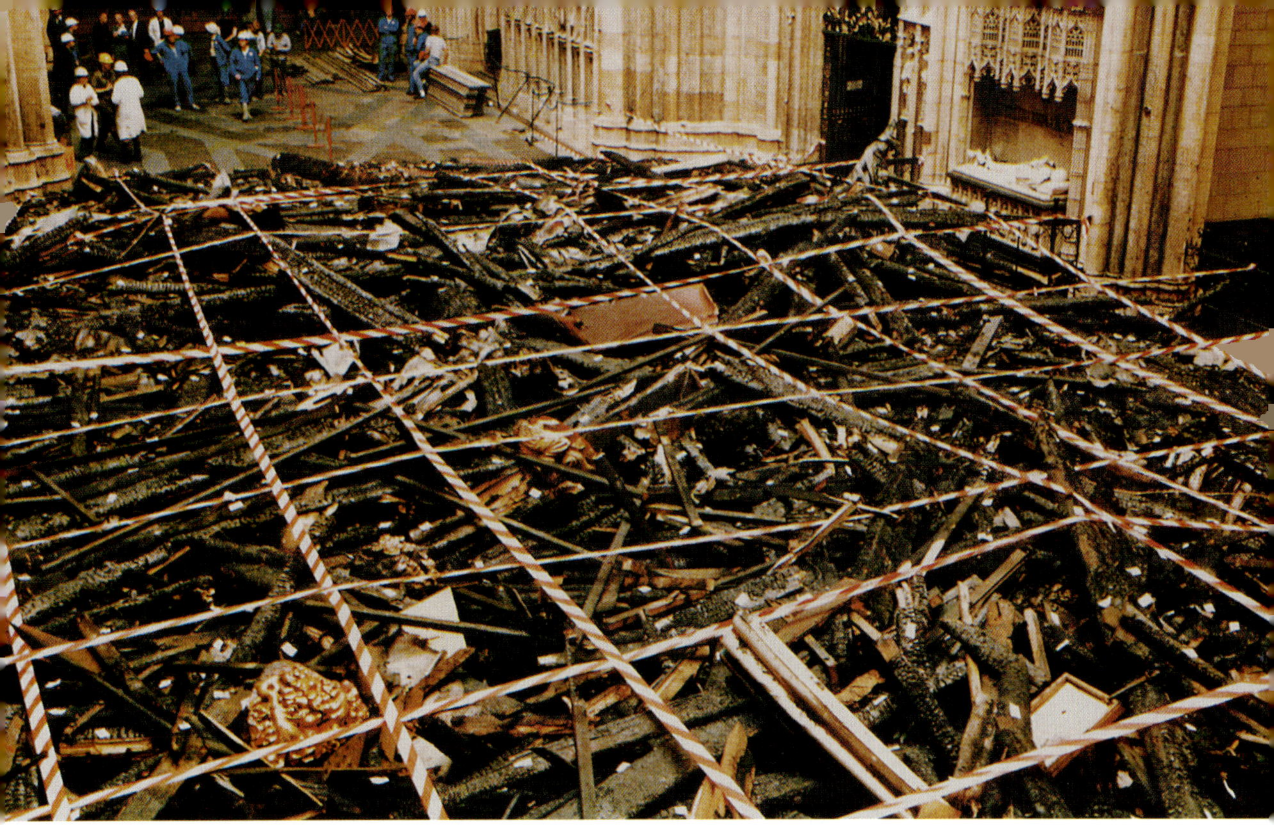

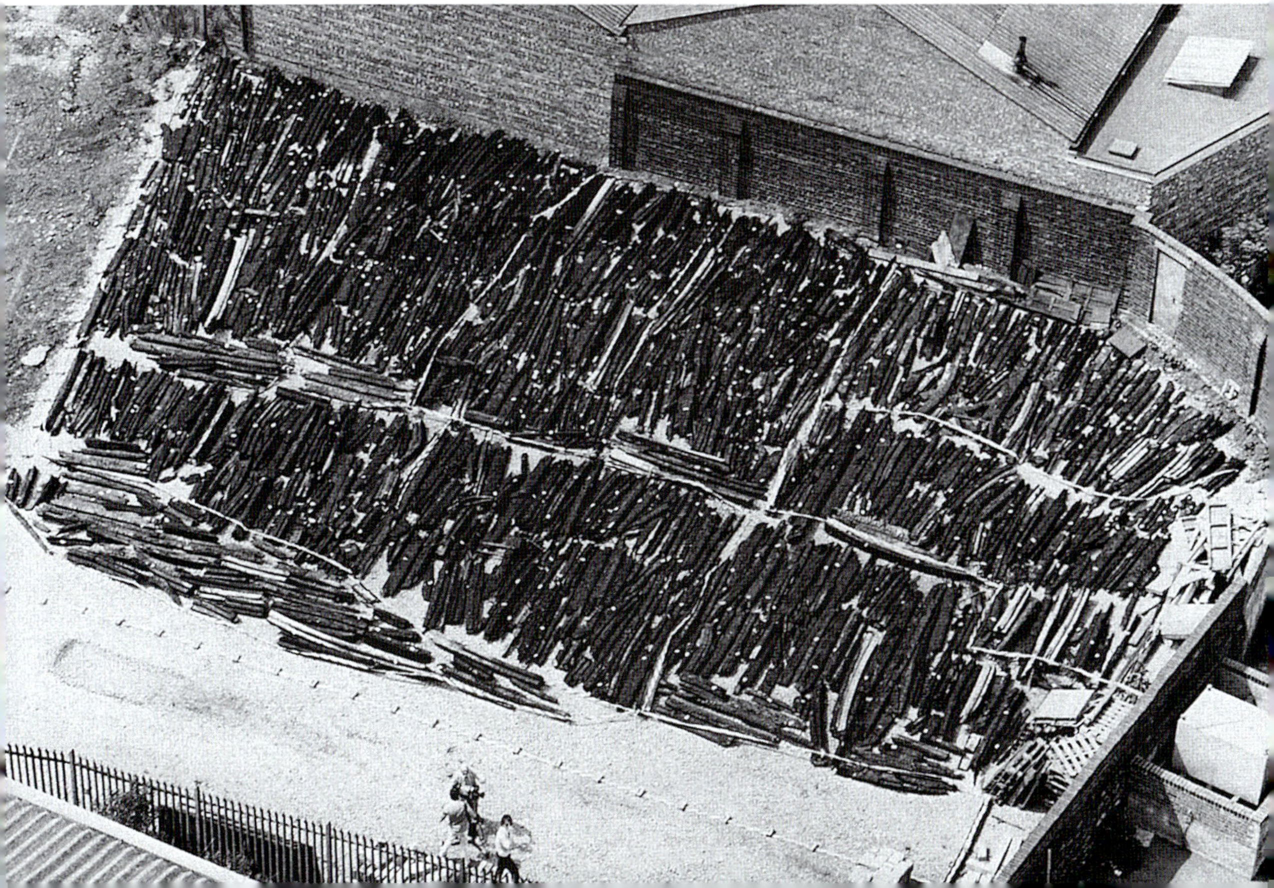

the vault. In 1978, it was found that there had been serious death-watch beetle attack upon the vault, and 16 bosses and several ribs were replaced. The wood chosen for the replacement bosses was not oak but lime, and these new bosses withstood the flames better than the originals.

It is a sad irony, but the greatest advances in our knowledge of the structure of York Minster have come upon the heels of disaster. The fires of 1829 and 1840 led to quite extensive excavation, whilst the threat of the Minster's collapse in 1967 saw the beginning of a programme of archaeological excavation which continues to add greatly to our knowledge of the Minster and the site upon which it stands. It was the same with the fire of July 1984. For only when the charred timbers lay on the south transept floor did the 18th-century roof structure become accessible at last, allowing a full record to be made.

Once the timbers had cooled sufficiently to be handled, the matter of recording what remained became an orthodox archaeological exercise. The debris lay to a depth of 5 feet; the timber fragments found in it were numbered and then photographed within a reference grid. They were then removed to a site nearby where they could be examined more easily, and measured drawings could be made of details of the joints and rib profiles which survived. More than 1,000 fragments were recovered – so many that only an aerial photograph could include them all in one frame.

The fire at York Minster clearly demonstrated an interesting similarity between the recording procedures of archaeology and forensic science. Investigators into the cause of the fire paid close attention to the catalogue and plan of the fallen timbers compiled as the first stage of the archaeological record. Attention then turned to the fabric of the south transept itself where stonework, hidden between roof and vault until July 1984, now lay revealed. The survey of the structure greatly enhanced our understanding of the nature and phases of construction of the south transept – one of the most complex areas of the Minster – and its earlier repairs and restorations.

★

ABOVE: *The arch between the transept and the central tower, its stone reddened by heat and blackened by smoke.*

FACING PAGE, ABOVE: *One of the few bosses which survived the flames: an unusual theme, for most of the bosses were based upon foliate designs.*

FACING PAGE, BELOW: *A small part of the rose window, showing the network of cracks caused by the heat of the fire and the subsequent cooling.*

Restoration

Those present in York on the morning of Monday 9 July 1984 will never forget the horror and disbelief with which all contemplated the ruined transept. Particularly affected by the sight were the Minster craftsmen who only seven years previously had laboured to restore the timber vault with its carved and gilded bosses and ribs.

The horror was, however, overcome by intense relief and thankfulness that the damage was not worse, and that no one had been injured. Immediate action had to be taken to protect the Minster interior and, following the archaeological survey of the fallen timbers, clearance of the debris of the roof was commenced and timber and scaffolding screens erected to block off all the arches leading into the Minster. An army of volunteers cleaned the floors and furnishings, and so supreme was the effort of all that the nave of the Minster was opened on Wednesday morning and the cathedral restored for worship by the Sunday. On the days immediately following the fire the usual services had been moved to St Michael-le-Belfry nearby.

On the day of the fire, the first meeting took place of the team entrusted by the Dean and Chapter to oversee the restoration of the Minster and the construction of the new roof. This was led by the Surveyor of the Fabric and comprised the Superintendent of Works, his Deputy, the Structural Engineer, the Quantity Surveyor and the Bursar.

The first task was to ensure the well-being of the Minster by continuing the erection of the protective screens, and this was completed by a temporary roof over the transept, of reinforced plastic supported on lightweight metal trusses, which was in place three weeks after the fire. Secondly, it was essential to clean the Minster of the soot which had begun to settle over the entire interior. Apart from the disfigurement it produced, the soot was acidic and such a deposit could damage stone, glass, carpets and fabrics. The latter were removed or cleaned *in situ* and a programme of cleaning by vacuuming was started on all walls, windows and floors. Mercifully, as the fire occurred during a period of dry weather, the surfaces

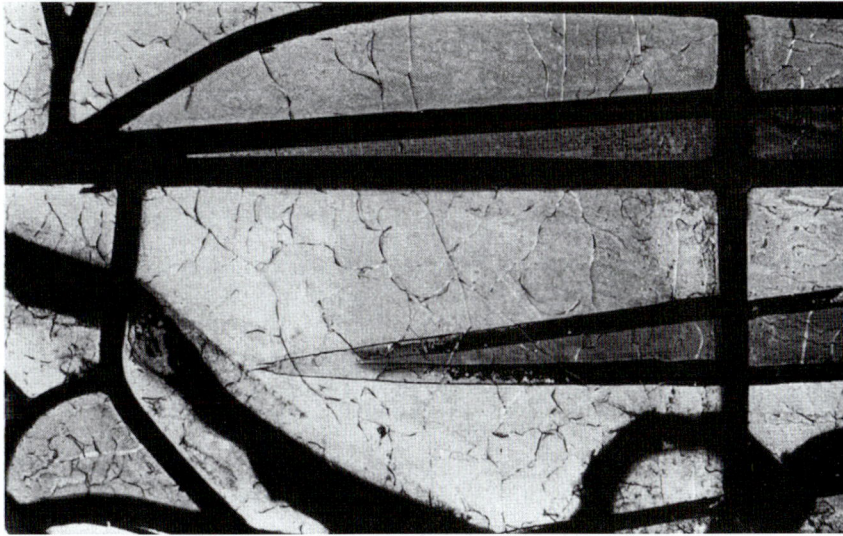

upon which the soot fell were very dry and the soot had settled gradually and loosely, most of it falling to the floor. Experts from the British Museum advised that it could be over nine months before the air had completely cleared and the soot settled.

Thirdly, the new Undercroft had to be rescued from the flooding caused by the water pouring into it. Remarkably, no exhibits were lost, for the water was quickly pumped out and some of it may have escaped through the still active Roman drains under the Minster. The organ had suffered some damage by water and soot, but apart from a thorough cleaning, little repair was necessary.

The team then assessed the amount of structural damage. The skill of the Fire Brigade had ensured that the destruction had been marvellously confined. The roof and vault had gone but the side walls were virtually undamaged, the transept aisles untouched, and even the stone floor, which received tons of burning timbers falling from nearly 100 feet, was only chipped in four places. Nevertheless, the stonework of the great south gable was damaged by the severe heat and the top of the great arch leading into the central tower was disfigured by shattered stones.

The stained glass of the transept was virtually undamaged, except for

the early 16th-century glass of the beautiful rose window. This had been cracked and crazed into thousands of pieces but most fortunately the window had been re-leaded 12 years earlier and no glass had fallen from it.

The safety of the great gable had to be checked and an inspection by the team was possible within a few days. The structure proved safe, and although many surface stones had been calcified and would have to be replaced, the heart of the seven-foot-thick wall was solid and firm, thanks to a repair carried out 100 years ago.

Scaffolding was erected swiftly and the glass and loose stone safely removed. The transept was filled with scaffolding supporting a large working area at the level of the vault, which quickly got the nickname 'the ball-room'. Corridors were formed through the scaffolding at ground level and the circulation routes of the Minster restored, including access to the Undercroft.

While these initial tasks were being carried out, the Project Team was also involved in very detailed consideration as to how a new roof and vault should be constructed. It was necessary, first of all, to establish whether the roof should be replaced at all. There had been suggestions that the area should be left as an impressive open space and a great window made to fill the transept arch. However, the concept was rejected; among other things, the Minster needs the floor space for seating on great occasions, and the delicate interior carvings of the transept would deteriorate if exposed to modern polluted outside air. The Chapter agreed with the team that the lead-covered roof should be replaced as before, with a vault visible from the interior. The original vault, introduced in the late 15th century to give the cathedral interior an aesthetic architectural unity, was to be recreated in general form as before, but would differ in some details.

Some of the original 68 bosses survived the fire and they would be refixed. The others would depict symbolically all those who so generously supported the rebuilding scheme by the gifts of materials (such as oak for the bosses and ribs) or money.

Careful thought was given to the material from which the vault was to be made. In medieval times, vaults of this design were normally constructed from stone, but at York the spans of the high vaults are so large (over 15 feet) that the stability of a stone vault was doubted and wood was employed instead. A reinforced stone vault could possibly have been constructed today, but its weight would have produced great strain on the existing walls. Other materials, for instance glass fibre, were considered but rejected, because either their inflammability was great or their anticipated life uncertain. It is important to stress that the Chapter required that only material with a proven life span should be employed and that, if possible, the whole roof (apart from the lead covering) should be planned to last at least 500 years! For this reason, the vault was to be constructed of timber but the infill panels were to be plaster, as in the nave and choir, to improve the vault's resistance to fire.

A more difficult decision was necessary over the materials to be used for the structure which helps to support the vault and totally supports the outer roof. This structure is invisible from inside or out, but is of course of vital importance. Reinforced concrete might have been suitable but its weight was a disadvantage and erection would not have been easy. The choice of material swiftly narrowed to either steel or timber. Careful study showed that protected steel could have greater fire resistance and its behaviour was predictable. Nevertheless, despite the unpredictable behaviour, particularly of green timber, and its lesser fire resistance, a timber roof, if carefully maintained, will last at least 500 years. Moreover, if the timbers were made larger than necessary, in the event of another fire the charring of the wood

★

FACING PAGE: *The roofless south transept (above), and filled with scaffolding (below).*

ABOVE RIGHT: *The blackened rose window with the first scaffolding built to provide access for inspection of the damage.*

RIGHT: *Beneath a temporary roof of steel tubing and translucent sheeting, the floor upon which the new vault would be assembled is carried upon scaffolding.*

would give protection against complete destruction. The outcome of all the research and consultation was therefore that the roof structure was also to be in timber – oak, in fact, which was available in the necessary size and lengths.

It was also decided that both the roof and vault were to be constructed by the Minster craftsmen, for within that body of men there was the expertise and talent to understand the great task. The huge oak frames would be made in a temporary workshop in Deans Park, transported by crane to Deangate and lifted by a larger crane to their final position. Meanwhile the stone repairs, undertaken at the Minster Stoneyard and involving much careful carving, would be completed, all beneath a second temporary plastic roof. Work would also continue on the construction of the vault and the repairing of the cracked glass. The latter would be saved by sandwiching it between two sheets of clear glass after careful cleaning. The new roof was completed in 1986, but the extensive carving for the vault was not completed until 1988 when a service of re-dedication was held, attended by Her Majesty The Queen.

The fire destroyed 10 per cent of the Minster's vulnerable timber roofs, always the victims of the fires the Minster suffered. In order to try and ensure as far as humanely possible that no more fires occur, highly sophisticated detection and protection systems now guard against fire and lightning. The rose window is protected from erosion and pollution by its glass 'sandwich' and the stonework is restored to its former glory.

The intention in restoring the transept was that the finest craftsmanship of the day would surpass even that which was lost, and the transept today stands as testament to that.

The latter Glory of this House shall be greater than the former saith the Lord of Hosts and in this place will I give peace.
Hag: 2:10